Good Question!

What Was Your Dream, Dr. King?
AND OTHER QUESTIONS ABOUT. . .
Martin Luther King Jr.

STERLING CHILDREN'S BOOKS
New York

STERLING CHILDREN'S BOOKS
New York

An Imprint of Sterling Publishing
387 Park Avenue South
New York, NY 10016

Text © 2013 Mary Kay Carson
Illustrations by Jim Madsen © 2013 Sterling Publishing Co., Inc.
Design by Elizabeth Phillips
Photo Credits: Corbis: 27 © David J. & Janice L. Frent Collection; Getty Images: 5, Hulton Archive

Page 5 "I have a dream today!" Martin Luther King Jr. "I Have a Dream" speech delivered August 28, 1963, at the Lincoln Memorial, Washington, D.C.
[transcription/audio: http://www.americanrhetoric.com/speeches/mlkihaveadream.htm]
Page 12 "You may do that." Juan Williams. *Eyes on the Prize: America's Civil Rights Years, 1954–1965.* (New York: Penguin Books, 2002), 66.
Page 17 "No matter . . . with nonviolence," Martin Luther King, Jr. *Stride Toward Freedom: The Montgomery Story.* (Boston: Beacon Press, 2010), 128.
Page 21 "Nonviolent resistance is not a method for cowards," Ibid., 90.
Page 21 "[W]hen you . . . to wait." Martin Luther King, Jr. *Why We Can't Wait.* (Boston: Beacon Press, 2011).
Page 22 "I have a dream today!" Martin Luther King Jr. "I Have a Dream" speech delivered August 28, 1963, at the Lincoln Memorial, Washington, D.C.
[transcription/audio: http://www.americanrhetoric.com/speeches/mlkihaveadream.htm]
Page 27 "I believe. . . movements." Garrow, David J. *Bearing the Cross: Martin Luther King, Jr., and the Southern Christian Leadership Conference.* (New York: HarperCollins, 2004).
Page 30 "What are you doing for others?" *I Have A Dream: The Quotations Of Martin Luther King, Jr.* (New York: Grosset & Dunlap, 1968), 2.

ISBN 978-1-4027-9622-7 (hardcover)
ISBN 978-1-4027-9045-4 (paperback)

Library of Congress Cataloging-in-Publication Data

Carson, Mary Kay.
 What was your dream, Dr. King? : and other questions about Martin Luther King, Jr. / by Mary Kay Carson.
  p. cm.
 ISBN 978-1-4027-9622-7 (hardcover) -- ISBN 978-1-4027-9045-4 (pbk.) 1. King, Martin Luther Jr., 1929-1968--Juvenile
 literature. 2. African Americans--Biography--Juvenile literature. 3. Civil rights workers--United States--Biography-
 -Juvenile literature. 4. Baptists--United States--Clergy--Biography--Juvenile literature. 5. African Americans-
 -Civil rights--History--20th century--Juvenile literature. I. Title.
 E185.97.K5C36 2013
 323.092--dc23
 [B]

                                2012021259

Distributed in Canada by Sterling Publishing
c/o Canadian Manda Group, 165 Dufferin Street
Toronto, Ontario, Canada M6K 3H6
Distributed in the United Kingdom by GMC Distribution Services
Castle Place, 166 High Street, Lewes, East Sussex, England BN7 1XU
Distributed in Australia by Capricorn Link (Australia) Pty. Ltd.
P.O. Box 704, Windsor, NSW 2756, Australia

For information about custom editions, special sales, and premium and corporate purchases,
please contact Sterling Special Sales at 800-805-5489 or specialsales@sterlingpublishing.com.

Manufactured in China
Lot #:
2 4 6 8 10 9 7 5 3 1
10/12

www.sterlingpublishing.com/kids

CONTENTS

Martin Luther King Jr. accepts the Nobel Peace Prize.

What was your dream, Dr. King?

Martin Luther King Jr. looked out into a sea of people. More than two hundred thousand people crowded into the National Mall in Washington, DC. They traveled from all over the nation. On that hot August afternoon in 1963, King stood on the steps of the Lincoln Memorial. He looked cool and calm as he began to speak. King delivered an unforgettable speech that day. His words electrified and inspired his audience.

Dr. King told the crowd that this was a difficult time for America, but that he had hope for a better future. "I have a dream today!" Dr. King said. He explained that his dream was that all people would someday be treated fairly. He dreamed that people wouldn't be judged by the color of their skin. King looked forward to a day when children of different races would learn and play together. His dream was for a different world. He wanted love, understanding, and peace to be more powerful than hate, ignorance, and war. When he finished speaking, the crowd cheered and clapped.

Martin Luther King Jr. was a famous leader. He helped bring rights, equality, and fair treatment to millions of African Americans. Dr. King and his dream forever changed the United States of America.

Martin Luther King Jr. delivers his "I Have a Dream" speech.

Why couldn't young Martin go to the same restaurants, swimming pools, and schools as other children?

Martin learned as a young boy that skin color separated people. He grew up seeing "Whites Only" signs at swimming pools and restaurants. He used water fountains and restrooms that were seperated by race. A six-year-old neighborhood boy told Martin he couldn't play with him anymore. Why not? The friend had started school. Only white kids like him could go there. Martin was African American, so he went to a separate school. The boy's parents no longer let him play with Martin or other black kids.

This was what life was like in Georgia when Martin was a young boy in the 1930s. Laws kept African Americans separated from white people. It was called segregation. Where you could live, go to school, shop, eat, and work depended on your skin color. Segregation laws made life harder for African Americans. The best jobs weren't open to them. Black schools had fewer teachers and books. Many stores, restaurants, and swimming pools had signs saying "Whites Only." Black people were treated unfairly. They had to sit at the back of the bus. They often had to use the back door when entering stores or white homes.

Why was segregation allowed? Keeping people separate by race started with slavery. Enslaving black people was legal in the southern United States until the Civil War. Dr. King's great-grandfather was owned by a white person. Slaves were property, bought and sold just like tools, houses, or horses. Many whites believed dark-skinned people were different and that white people were better, or superior, so slavery wasn't wrong. White superiority didn't disappear when slavery ended in 1865. Southern states quickly passed laws to keep the races separate.

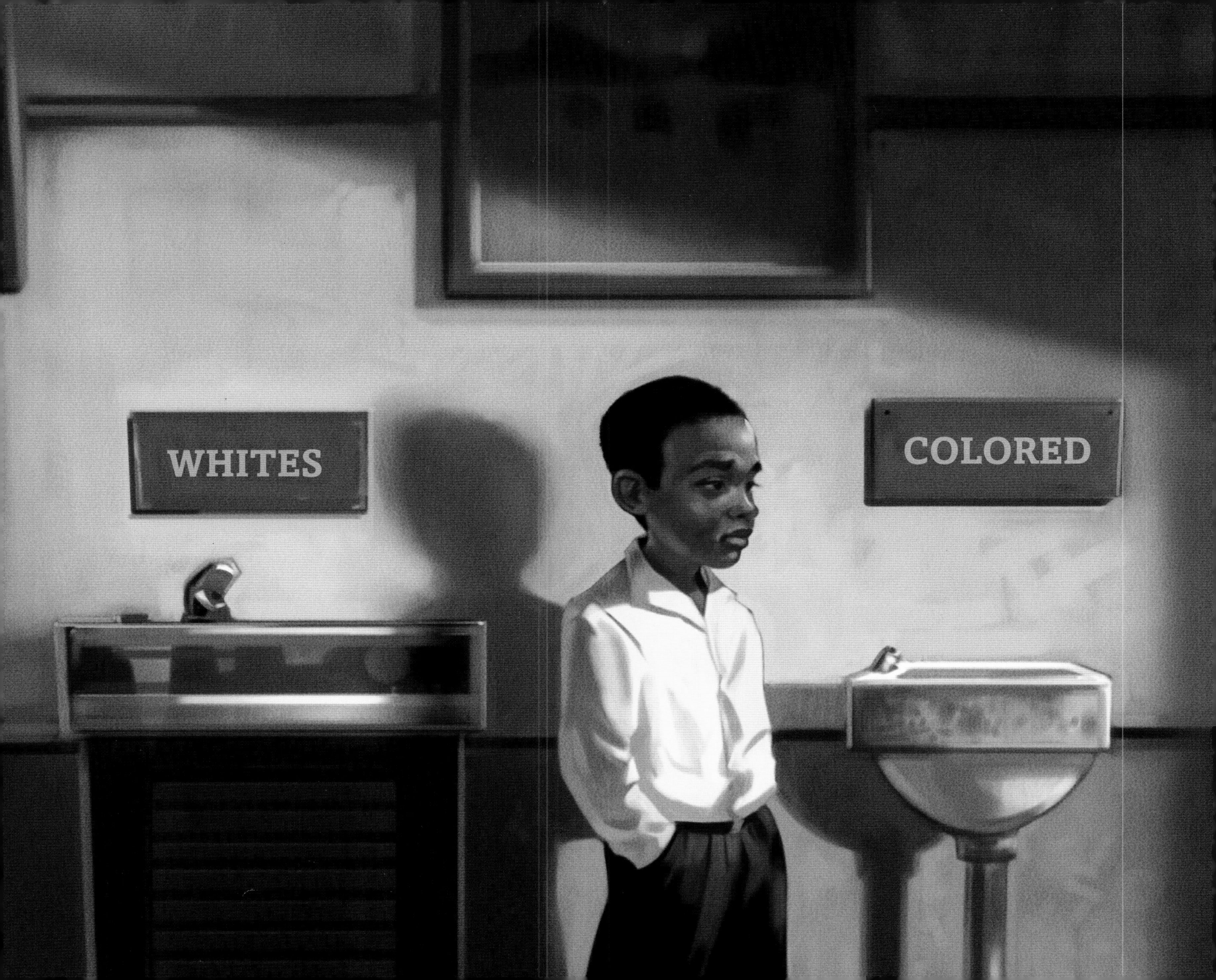
WHITES
COLORED

What gave Martin confidence and courage?

Segregation made Martin feel less important than whites. Martin and his brother and sister weren't worthy of a school as good as the school for white kids. African American fathers weren't worth the same pay as white dads. African American mothers had to use the back door of stores. These were the messages segregation threw at young Martin. But he didn't believe them. The King family knew better and made sure Martin did, too.

Both of Martin's parents went to college. His mother was a schoolteacher. Alberta King told her son again and again in a hundred ways: You're as good as anybody else. Martin's father was the minister of an important church. Reverend Martin Luther King Sr. was a leader in the community. He thought segregation was unfair and spoke out against it. The comfortable King home was full of family. Ideas, words, and music lived there, too. Martin grew up hearing powerful sermons.

At fourteen, Martin won a speech contest. On their way home, Martin and his teacher had to give up their bus seats to white passengers. They stood for the ninety-mile journey. Martin was angrier than he'd ever been in his whole life. He knew he was as good as anybody else— his heart and brain told him so! But the world treated him as if he wasn't. Was he wrong? Or was the world wrong? There's nothing wrong with me, thought Martin. Segregation is what's wrong. And somebody needs to fix that.

What kind of doctor was Dr. King?

Martin Luther King Jr. wasn't a medical doctor. His title comes from earning a very advanced degree in school. Martin skipped the ninth and twelfth grades and went to Morehouse College in Atlanta, Georgia. It was a college for black men only. Martin's father, Reverend King, had gone there, too.

A summer farm job in Connecticut helped young King find his path. It was Martin's first trip out of the segregated South. In Connecticut he ate at any restaurant he wanted. He could sit in the front row at the movies. It was a glimpse into a different world—one where people of different races lived together. On the train ride back to Atlanta, King was reminded of the differences. When the train reached the South he had to move to a car for black people. And when he went to eat, a waiter sat him in the back of the dining car. Then he pulled a curtain, separating King from white diners.

Martin wanted to help African Americans suffering under segregation. So he decided to become a minister like his father. Eventually he earned a degree from Boston University that gave him the title "doctor" of religion, which is why he's called Dr. King.

Did Dr. King have kids?

Martin Luther King Jr. married Coretta Scott in 1953. She was a music student from Alabama. The couple eventually had four children. The oldest was a daughter, Yolanda. Two sons, Martin and Dexter, were born next. Another daughter, Bernice, was the last. Yolanda was born in 1955, soon after Dr. King became the minister of a church in Montgomery, Alabama.

Who was Rosa Parks?

Rosa Parks was a seamstress in Montgomery, Alabama. On the evening of December 1, 1955, Parks was riding the bus home. She was in the back, where African Americans like her had to sit. When more passengers boarded the bus, the front filled up. The bus driver told Parks to give her seat to a white man. She stayed seated. The driver threatened to have her arrested. "You may do that," was all she said. Two policemen came and took her to jail.

African American leaders in Montgomery wanted to protest Rosa Parks's arrest. Let's stop paying money to a bus company that treats us unfairly, they argued. Protestors decided to boycott, or refuse to ride, the buses. The bus company relied on fares from black riders. Without their money, the city's public bus system would be in trouble. On the day of Parks's trial, African Americans stayed off city buses. The Montgomery bus boycott was on. Organizers chose twenty-six-year-old Martin Luther King Jr. to lead the boycott. King organized carpools and gave speeches.

In addition to the boycott, black community leaders also challenged the Montgomery bus segregation laws in court. These actions made many white people angry. They threatened Dr. King. Someone threw a bomb at his home. Thankfully, no one was hurt.

The boycotters won their victory in court after a year of protesting. In 1956, the U.S. Supreme Court forced Montgomery's buses to undo segregation, or desegregate. Bus boycotts soon spread to other Southern cities. African Americans across the South began organizing. They wanted the same rights as everyone else. These rights are called civil rights and they protect peoples' freedoms. African Americans wanted the right to live and work anywhere, and to receive equal public services, like good schools. It was the beginning of a movement—the civil rights movement. And its leader was Martin Luther King Jr.

Did the South try to end segregation?

Segregation was centuries old. Desegregating schools, movie theaters, and buses would change life in the South. Many white people didn't want things to change. They believed that different races should stay separated. Supporters of segregation didn't feel that others should be able to tell them how to live. Some restaurant and store owners refused to serve African Americans. Many local and state governments tried to block desegregation. Southerners didn't want the courts, federal government, and other outsiders ordering them around. Segregation wasn't going to end easily.

Central High was a white school in Little Rock, Arkansas. In 1957, courts ordered the school to accept black students. Arkansas's governor refused. He sent the Arkansas National Guard to the school. Armed with weapons, these soldiers kept African American students from entering. So President Eisenhower sent in U.S. Army soldiers. The soldiers protected nine black students so they could study at Central High.

Everyday life became extra difficult for African Americans in the South. Even speaking out against segregation might get them fired. No one wants to hire a "troublemaker." Joining the civil rights movement made them targets. White hate groups like the Klu Klux Klan terrorized black communities. Klan members wore white hoods and robes to disguise themselves. They burned homes, beat people up, and killed them, too. Who could you go to for help? Many governors, police, and other officials were against desegregation. Deciding to speak out was risky—for yourself, your livelihood, and your family.

How did civil rights workers protest peacefully?

Angry neighbors and supporters gathered outside Dr. King's home. The Montgomery bus boycott was on, and someone had just bombed his house. White police officers showed up. Would there be a riot? Dr. King walked out onto his ruined porch. The crowd got quiet. "If you have weapons, take them home," said King. "We must love our white brothers," the Baptist minister reminded them. "No matter what they do to us." Revenge wasn't the answer. "We must meet violence with nonviolence," King said.

Dr. King believed violence was wrong. He thought that hurting people would only create enemies, not solve problems. We can't make the world better with guns and fists, he argued. Only nonviolent action would work. Dr. King had studied the work of Gandhi. Gandhi's nonviolent protests helped to earn India its freedom from Great Britain without war.

So how do you fight peacefully? You break laws you think are wrong—on purpose and in public. And if you get into trouble for breaking the law, you don't run away or fight back. Instead, you face the consequences, so others see that it's wrong. This way of acting is called civil disobedience.

Civil disobedience was the weapon of civil rights workers. Like Rosa Parks, they chose not to obey laws they believed wrong. Civil rights protestors broke all kinds of segregation laws. African Americans were arrested for using "Whites Only" drinking fountains. Police took white protestors to jail for riding in the back of the bus. Black college students sat at tables and lunch counters in diners that only served whites. Groups of black and white people boarded public buses together in the segregated South. They called themselves Freedom Riders. When Freedom Riders stopped at bus stations, black passengers sat in "white" waiting rooms and white riders used restrooms set aside for African Americans.

How did Dr. King convince America that segregation was wrong?

Dr. King traveled around the South to join protests and lead marches. He prayed with marchers and sang their battle hymn: "We shall overcome. . . . We shall overcome some day. . ."

Protesters were committed to nonviolence. But those against them were not. Civil rights workers had to stay calm when spat at and called horrible names. They learned to protect themselves when kicked and beaten by police officers. "Nonviolent resistance is not a method for cowards," King said. The civil rights movement forced America to think about a shameful part of its history. Segregation wasn't just a Southern tradition. It came from slavery's belief in white superiority—that black people don't deserve equal treatment

Americans were realizing that segregation was simply wrong—and illegal. Skin color doesn't determine the civil rights of a U.S. citizen. Watching news reports of what was happening changed many minds. Americans saw shocking pictures of bleeding peaceful protestors beaten by police officers. They saw angry white Southerners screaming terrible names at black school children. While a stunned nation watched, America came to know Dr. King. He seemed to always say exactly what was needed—whether to bring calm, lift spirits, or perfectly explain a point. Thanks to Dr. King and the civil rights movement, segregation was no longer the South's problem. It became America's problem.

Why did Dr. King go to jail?

In 1963, all of America watched Dr. King working in Birmingham, Alabama. The backlash against ending segregation there was violent. White hate groups had bombed seventeen African American churches. The city was becoming known as Bombingham, Alabama. In April, civil rights workers began protests there. African Americans sat at "Whites Only" lunch counters. Dr. King led a march to desegregate department stores that had separate white bathrooms and wouldn't hire black workers. Police turned attack dogs and powerful hoses on marchers. They filled jails for miles around with protestors—including Dr. King.

During King's time in jail, Birmingham's white clergymen criticized King's methods. They asked African Americans not to protest but to wait for courts to change laws. Dr. King wrote them a letter, using whatever scraps of paper he could find in his cell. "[W]hen you have seen vicious mobs lynch your mothers and fathers . . . and . . . when you have seen hate-filled policemen curse, kick and even kill your black brothers and sisters; . . . then you will understand why we find it difficult to wait." Newspapers printed King's "Letter from Birmingham City Jail." Americans across the country read it. More and more people understood the need for change.

Did kids protest for civil rights, too?

Kids as young as six marched in Birmingham that spring. More than a thousand young people took part in the Children's Crusade. Police arrested so many kids, they used school buses to take them to jail. Firefighters used powerful hoses to slam kids against trees and cars. Police dogs attacked crowds and bit marchers. The pictures and television images of the Children's Crusade horrified America. They sent letters to the president about it. Many joined the civil rights movement—black and white people, Southern and Northern.

Why did 250,000 people march for freedom?

Dr. King knew that African Americans needed new laws to end segregation and protect civil rights. It was time the entire country knew that. To get the message out, King and other leaders organized a March on Washington. On August 28, 1963, about 250,000 people went to the U.S. capital. People of all colors, ages, and religions marched with Dr. King that warm summer day. They listened to speeches given from the steps of the Lincoln Memorial.

Martin Luther King Jr. spoke last. "I have a dream today!" Dr. King told the crowd. "I have a dream that one day this nation will rise up and live out the true meaning of its creed: We hold these truths to be self-evident: that all men are created equal." Listeners shouted, whistled, and clapped their agreement. But Dr. King wasn't finished.

"I have a dream. That one day on the red hills of Georgia, the sons of former slaves and the sons of former slave owners will be able to sit down together at the table of brotherhood," he continued. "I have a dream that my four little children will one day live in a nation where they will not be judged by the color of their skin," he said, "but by the content of their character." By sharing his dreams, King gave others the courage to dream, too.

What is the Civil Rights Act?

While in D.C. that day, Dr. King visited members of Congress and the president. He asked them to vote for a law. They did. The Civil Rights Act of 1964 ended segregation in public places like parks, playgrounds, and libraries. Under the new law, hotels, theaters, and restaurants must admit black customers and women. Schools and jobs had to be open to men and women of all races. The Civil Rights Act changed America. People around the world admired Dr. King and his nonviolent fight.

Could African Americans in the South vote?

Yes, but few were registered. All Americans have to sign up, or register, before voting. In the 1960s, voters registered at local government offices. In the South, workers at these offices often tried to keep African Americans from signing up to vote. They would insult or threaten black voters. They would force them to pay a tax or take a writing test. White voters weren't asked to do these things. The Civil Rights Act outlawed segregation, but it didn't protect voters' rights. Dr. King knew that voting is power. Voting rights became the next battle.

Alabama was the place to start. The town of Selma, for example, was home to approximately 15,000 African Americans, but only 150 could vote. In 1965, Dr. King helped an effort to sign up black voters in Alabama. But civil rights workers met with trouble when they tried marching to the state capital of Montgomery. Police attacked them with tear gas and billy clubs. So many people were hurt that March 7, 1965, was named "Bloody Sunday."

President Lyndon B. Johnson called it an American tragedy. He told the nation that everyone must work to overcome prejudice and racism. "And we *shall* overcome," he said. President Johnson was from the South, so his words were extra meaningful.

Dr. King continued the fight in Selma. He walked with thousands of marchers to Alabama's capital. President Johnson sent soldiers to protect them. From March 21 to 25, thousands marched toward Montgomery. Freedom marchers camped out in tents at night along the way. People from across the country joined them. More than 25,000 marchers walked the last six miles. Alabama's governor refused to talk to Dr. King, but it didn't matter. The U.S. Congress passed a national law, the Voting Rights Act of 1965. Dr. King and Rosa Parks were with President Johnson when he signed it into law.

Protestors with the Poor People's Campaign camped out in Washington, D.C.

Did Dr. King continue fighting?

The civil rights movement ended segregation and won rights for voters. But there was plenty of unfairness toward African Americans outside the South, too. Racism kept neighborhoods, workplaces, and schools separated by skin color. Black people were turned away when trying to rent or buy homes in white neighborhoods. White bosses didn't hire African American workers. Many black families lived in terrible poverty in Northern cities. Martin Luther King Jr. knew he had more work to do. His dream of fairness included not being poor. This meant a decent place to live, good schools, and jobs for people of every color. Dr. King began planning another march on Washington. It would be called the Poor People's Campaign.

Dr. King also dreamed of peace. By the spring of 1967, he was speaking out against the Vietnam War. Thousands of American soldiers were dying in the war. And so were Vietnamese people. "I believe everyone has a duty to be in both the civil rights and peace movements," said King.

King's peaceful and prayerful methods didn't make sense to everyone. Some young black protesters felt that change was too slow. And why shouldn't they fight violence with violence? Some supporters of Dr. King's civil rights movement did not agree with his fight against poverty or the Vietnam War. These ideas were too radical, they said.

What happened to Dr. King?

The world will never know what more Dr. King could have accomplished. What other dreams might he have fought for? Sadly, Martin Luther King Jr. died on April 4, 1968. He was only thirty-nine years old. King was shot and murdered outside his motel room in Memphis, Tennessee. Dr. King was in Memphis to march with black garbage collectors. The men were on strike because they earned less than white workers. Dr. King went to help change that unfairness.

Martin Luther King Jr.'s work did not die with him. Within days of his funeral, Coretta Scott King was back in Memphis marching with the garbage workers. They got a pay raise. King's widow spoke in her husband's place at a rally against the Vietnam War. Mrs. King also stood in for him on the steps of the Lincoln Memorial during the Poor People's Campaign march.

Who killed Dr. King?

James Earl Ray was a criminal. He escaped from prison in 1967. A year later, Ray read about King's visit to Tennessee in the newspaper. Ray traveled to Memphis and rented a room that overlooked King's motel. Then he waited and watched from his window while holding a rifle. He shot when King stepped onto the motel balcony. Ray believed that whites were superior to African Americans. He didn't like black people voting or gaining power. James Earl Ray spent the rest of his life in prison for Dr. King's murder.

How do we honor Dr. King and his work?

The dreams of Martin Luther King Jr. are still alive. His life story, work, and words inspire people everyday. A national holiday honors him every year on the third Monday in January. Martin Luther King Jr. Day falls each year near Dr. King's birthday, January 15. King said that life is always asking: "What are you doing for others?" Many Americans remember his life of service by helping their neighbors and communities on his national holiday.

Coretta Scott King helped to preserve her husband's work and legacy with the King Center in Atlanta. Unfortunately, she died before the Martin Luther King Jr. Memorial was finished in Washington, D.C. It opened on the National Mall in 2011. Visitors take a path through the huge stone Mountain of Despair. While they are walking, another huge rock, called the Stone of Hope, is in view. On the stone's other side is carved a giant statue of Martin Luther King Jr., where he stands with his arms crossed. His gaze goes over the visitors, out toward open water.

Has Dr. King's dream come true?

The America that Martin Luther King Jr. grew up in is different today. White and black children go to school together. Segregation is illegal. It is a crime to turn someone down for a job because of race. An African American man, Barack Obama, became president in 2008. Our nation has come a long way.

Not all people everywhere are always treated fairly, however. The world in King's "I Have a Dream" speech hasn't come completely true. There is still prejudice, poverty, and war. He knew it would take time and not be easy. But Martin Luther King Jr. believed the world could—and would—become a better place. All that is needed is for us to believe in his dream, too.

MARTIN LUTHER KING JR. TIMELINE

1929 Martin Luther King Jr. is born in Atlanta, Georgia.

1948 King graduates college and becomes a minister at age 19.

1953 Marries music student Coretta Scott.

1954 King becomes minister of Dexter Avenue Baptist Church in Montgomery, Alabama.

1955 Receives a PhD in religious studies from Boston University.
King leads the boycott of segregated buses in Montgomery, Alabama.

1956 King's house is bombed during the Montgomery bus boycott.
U.S. Supreme Court ruling forces Montgomery to desegregate city buses.

1960 Moves to Atlanta and joins his father at Ebenezer Baptist Church.

1963 King is arrested and jailed during civil rights protests in Birmingham, Alabama.
Writes "Letter from Birmingham City Jail."
Delivers "I Have a Dream" speech during the March on Washington.

1964 U.S. Congress passes Civil Rights Act of 1964, outlawing segregation.
King receives Nobel Peace Prize.

1965 King joins voting rights march from Selma to Montgomery.
U.S. Congress passes Voting Rights Act of 1965.

1967 King begins speaking out against the Vietnam War.
He plans the Poor People's Campaign march on Washington.

1968 Martin Luther King Jr. is murdered in Memphis.

For bibliography and further reading visit: http://www.sterlingpublishing.com/kids/good-question